John T. King

Atlantic City as a Winter Sanitarium

John T. King

Atlantic City as a Winter Sanitarium

ISBN/EAN: 9783337253387

Printed in Europe, USA, Canada, Australia, Japan

Cover: Foto ©Andreas Hilbeck / pixelio.de

More available books at **www.hansebooks.com**

➤⁘JUST WHAT IS NEEDED BY THE MEDICAL PROFESSION.⁘➤

Extract of Malt and Hops in a Fluid State.

NOT TOO SWEET AND CLOVING.　　　　　　NOT THICK LIKE TAFFY.

Your attention is respectfully directed to

DUKEHART & CO.'S
Pure Fluid Extract of Malt and Hops

AND COMBINATIONS.

This elegant preparation is submitted to the Medical Profession as representing a result heretofore unattained in the manufacture of Malt Extracts, being a highly concentrated *Fluid* extract of proper consistency for mixing promptly with water or milk, yet free from alcohol and not liable to ferment. We claim that it is richer in diastase and in the specific nutriments of malt and hops than any extract in the market. To mothers nursing, with a deficiency of milk, it is of the greatest service. **Retail Price, 50 Cts.**

Niemeyer's Emulsion. Extract of Malt and Cod-Liver Oil,

Contains forty per cent. of best Cod Liver Oil and the soluble hypophosphites of Lime, Soda and Potash, THREE grains of the combined salts to the tablespoonful, ten per cent. of Glycerine and fifty per cent. of the Fluid Extract of Malt and Hops. We have evidence from the experience of physicians and others that it is the most easily assimilable form of Cod Liver Oil yet introduced to the Medical Profession. It is a perfect Emulsion, mixing readily with water, if desirable and is well fitted for administering to children and persons whose stomachs are too sensitive to retain the simple oil. Dose—Tablespoonful three times daily. Half this quantity for children. **Retail Price, 75 Cents.**

Extract of Malt and Hops with Hypophosphites.

Three grains to the tablespoonful in perfect solution. Dose one to two tablespoonsful three times a day. **Retail Price, 75 Cents.**

Malt, Wine, and Iron.

This combination consists of two parts Extract of Malt and Hops, and one part pure Imported Sherry Wine and four grains to the tablespoonful of Ammonia Citrate of Iron in solution. Dose.—A tablespoonful three times daily. **Retail Price, 75 Cents.**

Extract of Malt with Citrate of Iron and Quinia.

Extract of Malt and four grains to the tablespoonful of the soluble CITRATE OF IRON AND QUINIA. Dose—A tablespoonful three times daily. **Retail Price, $1.00.**

Physicians will be highly gratified at the results of a trial of any of the above preparations in cases where indicated, and their fluidity makes their administration easy and agreeable. For sale by all Druggists. Respectfully,

DUKEHART & CO., BALTIMORE, MD.

Important to Physicians and Invalids.

⇒❖ DUKEHART'S ⚜ PORTER ❖⇐

The superior quality and absolute purity of this porter causes it to be especially desirable as a tonic and mild stimulant for the debilitated and invalids. On account of these valuable properties it has entirely displaced beer and all other malt liquors for general use or medicinal purposes. A wine glass may be taken when desirable, at meals, or at intervals during the day.

The ingredients of this superior Porter are specially selected as to their purity and perfection, and the process of manufacture is cautiously observed. It is especially manufactured as a medicinal tonic for the invalid, and is stored in subterranean vaults of a uniform temperature the year round. This Porter is not surpassed in purity and superior qualities by any Porter manufactured in England or this country.

It is bottled with great care for medicinal use only, exclusively by EMILE SINSZ, Pharmacist, Corner Pennsylvania Avenue and Mosher St.; Corner Fremont and Townsend Sts.; and Corner Patterson Avenue and Stricker Street, Baltimore, Md.

Orders for this superior Porter will receive prompt attention, and sent by express or otherwise.

The Anglo-Swiss Condensed Milk Co., of Cham, Switzerland, the largest manufacturers of Condensed Milk in the world, having discovered a superior method of combining milk and cereal foods, have began the manufacture of a reliable food for infants and invalids. In order that the medical profession and others interested may know precisely what the constituent parts of this preparation are, a chemical analysis is printed upon the label of every can. Persons interested are invited to try this article and compare the results with those obtained from other foods. The advantages offered by the Anglo-Swiss Company are scientific preparation upon a large scale, thus assuring superior quality at a reasonable price. The name is

ANGLO-SWISS MILK FOOD.

The *Anglo-Swiss* brand of Condensed Milk is also a superior article: *twenty-five millions of cans sold in 1880.*

———

Ask your Druggist or Grocer for one of the little pamphlets issued by the Anglo-Swiss Company, telling how Condensed Milk and Milk Food should be prepared for infants. It has saved many lives.

☞The starchy condiments, ordinarily objectionable in Infants Food, are changed to Dextrine and Sugar, and rendered soluble and easily digestible by heating Anglo-Swiss Milk Food.

The Trade Supplied by H. K. & F. B. Thurber & Co. N. Y.

who will mail pamphlet if not obtainable elsewhere.

ATLANTIC CITY

AS A

WINTER SANITARIUM.

Its Geology, Climate, and Isothermal Relations,

AND

ITS SANITARY EFFECT

UPON DISEASES AND INVALIDS.

BALTIMORE:

G. H. JAMES & CO., FINE BOOK AND JOB PRINTERS,

No. 1 Mercer Street.

1881.

PHILADELPHIA TO ATLANTIC CITY AND CAPE MAY.

West Jersey Railroad

✦UNDER PENNSYLVANIA RAILROAD MANAGEMENT.✦

ROUTE.

Market St. Ferry to Camden, N. J.   Depot of West Jersey Railroad.

This road is under the management of the Pennsylvania Railroad and its construction, equipment, and service is in keeping with that world-famous perfection, safety, and comfort so eminently characteristic of that great Railroad Corporation. By this route the total distance from Philadelphia to Atlantic City is 64 miles. The track is laid with steel rails. The spaces between the ties are filled with gravel below the surface, thus effectually preventing any annoyance from dust at any season. It is equipped with Wharton switches; water tanks are laid between the rails by which the engine can be supplied with water without stopping the train. From Philadelphia to Atlantic City this route is a perfect AIR LINE! The schedule time from Philadelphia to Atlantic City is 1½ hours, with close connection with all Northern, Western, and Southern trains.

The West Jersey Railroad has erected at Atlantic City a large and ornate Excursion House for the accommodation of excursion parties, where every accommodation and comfort is furnished.

Baltimore & Philadelphia Steamboat Company.

1881.   Ericsson Line for Philadelphia.   1881.

The Steamers of this Company leave DAILY (Sunday excepted) at 3 P. M., from wharf corner Light and Pratt Streets. Cabin Fare, $2.00; Deck Fare, $1.50. Freight of all kinds taken at lowest rates.

J. ALEX. SHRIVER, Agent,

No. 3 Light St., Baltimore.

ATLANTIC CITY AS A WINTER SANITARIUM.

TO PHYSICIANS.

THE extraordinary sanitary benefit to be derived from a Winter's sojourn at Altantic City is so important to the invalid that the following pamphlet has been compiled for the information of Physicians and the benefit of Invalids.

This pamphlet will be sent gratuitously, postage paid, to a large number of Physicians all over the country.

Physicians to whom it is mailed will please acknowledge receipt.

ATLANTIC CITY.

THE SEA.

Thou glorious mirror, where the Almighty's form
Glasses itself in tempests; in all time
Calm or convulsed—in breeze, or gale or storm,
Icing the pole, or in the torrid clime
Dark-heaving;—boundless and sublime—
The image of eternity—the throne
Of the Invisible; even from out thy slime
The monsters of the deep are made; each zone
Obeys thee; thou goest forth, dread, fathomless, alone.

And I have loved thee, Ocean! and my joy
Of youthful sports was on thy breast
Born, like thy bubbles, onward: from a boy
I wantoned with thy breakers—they to me
Were a delight; and if the freshening sea
Made them a terror—'twas a pleasing fear,
For I was as it were a child of thee,
And trusted to thy billows far and near,
And laid my hand upon thy mane—as I do here.

How few realize that the sea is aught else than a lonely
boundless waste of water, to be regarded with dread, and
avoided with aversion.

Comparatively few contemplate it as the teeming abode
of millions of countless varieties of strange, wonderful, living
organisms, from the microscopic amorphous monad to the un-
wieldy leviathan, horrid octopus, and great whale.

The bed of the sea is the counterpart of the dry land. In
it are high mountains, and long valleys, and broad plateaus.

Upon many of these submarine plateaus the water is but a few feet in depth, while in the deep subaqueous valleys a depth of eight miles has been found.

What a vast expanse and varied home for the inhabitants of the sea! how wonderfully the Creator has adapted it to their nature! how fit an abiding place! Truly the bottom of the Atlantic Sea is diversified with mountain ranges and sublime precipices inconceivable in grandeur, with their perpendicular fall of water over ten miles in height and more than two thousand miles in breadth—from New Foundland to Ireland, and it is a demonstrable fact that there are vast submarine prairies constantly decked in gorgeous floral garniture, over which the great leviathan and whale and the lesser fishes disport and roam.

In some regions of the submarine continents crops of golden sheen and fructiferous vines grow in inconceivable luxuriance and wave upon the surface of the sea, for thousands of square miles, looking like a vast and boundless prairie of verdant garniture.

In the sea are immaculate coral mountains with perpendicular escarpments thousands of miles, in which are deep grottoes, caverns, and lofty arches, with innumerable coral pinnacles, and domes, that appear like the ornately chiseled façade of some vast and gorgeous cathedral, and the beholder would be fascinated and awed by beauty, magnitude, and grandeur, and would doubtingly ask—could this have been been built and so adorned by the insect world?

The sea is divided into three liquid strata or layers of water of different densities and properties. In the lowest stratum or deepest part of the sea we find the home of the crustacea, such as crabs, lobsters, and other like species; at a depth of five or six hundred feet we enter the domain of the invertebrate and vertebrate fishes and the various mollusks: in the third and superficial stratum we find minute animalculæ, mostly observable by the microscope.

To what provision of the Creator do the countless millions of the sea owe their existence and subsistence? What preserves the vast bulk of water and maintains its fitness for the support of animal life? Science shows that millions of tons of chloride of sodium or common salt is held in solution, and that it contains also vast quantities of magnesia and lime.

The innumerable currents and tides, and the continual agitation from winds that incessantly blow upon some portion of its surface, and the unceasing evaporation and uninterrupted contribution of rain from the clouds,—all these chemical and physical phenomena, with a thousand others, render the sea a fit and beautiful realm or abiding place for its inhabitants.

The color of the sea is not only a form of beauty, conveying pleasure to the mind, it is for an all-wise purpose. It is an indisputable fact that the color of the water of the sea is imparted to the fish which inhabit the particular locality, just as the plumage of birds corresponds to the foliage and forests they inhabit. Why is this? The similitude in color is a protection to them. They are not as noticeable, their presence is not as readily betrayed to their enemies as if they were of different color. Deep swimming fishes are invariably of bluish tint—for example, the well-known blue-fish. The parrot-fish is of a scarlet, as vivid as that of the birds in the forests of the neighboring land. The mullet is brilliant brown and gold, and the cod is invariably clad in Qauker gray. Thus these variously colored garbs of these piscatorial gentry of the sea are as multi-colored and as varied in cut as those of Broadway dandies or the Parisian exquisite.

The temperature of the sea for a certain depth corresponds to that of the atmosphere. At great depths the temperature falls almost to freezing point, and it is beyond question that the temperature of the sea has a like effect upon the monsters of the deep that it has upon the temperament of man. The barracuda of the tropic seas is as ferocious and savage as a tiger, and cannibal cruelty and voracity is eclipsed by that of the horrible, treacherous, and stealthy sea pirate, the " man-eating shark."

Not only does the sea furnish a vast home to the myriads of animals that live in its waters, it is the home of many of the feathered denizens of the air, especially of that beautiful, tiny, mysterious little bird known as "Mother Carey's chicken." This little bird is reared and makes its home upon the sea, thousands of miles from land. It daily, all day long, flits about incessantly; at night it roosts upon the raging billows, tucks its little head under its wing and goes to sleep amid the roar of the tempest and the fury of the blast. The great billow is its cradle and the seething foam its sheet. This little bird is safe and fearless, for He who holds these waters in the hollow of His hand, bids the tempest do them no harm.

The sea is the arena of the sublimest phosphorescent and pyrotechnic phenomena exhibited by wonderful nature. This phosphorescence is caused by countless millions of cyclidina, one 12,000th of an inch in length. It is not uncommon in tropic seas to see the phosphorescent current rushing past a ship in a band of light so luminous that one can easily read the time of night upon the face of a watch, and the billows, as they are dashed aside by the bow of a ship, look like broad sheets of ruddy flame. Especially is the great Gulf Stream the theatre of sublime electrical phenomena. For a continuous inexhaustible supply of fire-works and pyrotechnic beauties it is without a rival. It gives an exhibition upon the slightest occasion, and no ship ever crosses that wonderful tepid river of the sea, without being flooded with sheets of vivid lightning and a terrific bombardment from cloud batteries.

These are a few of the general beauties and wonders of the sea.

LAND AND SEA BREEZES.

No phenomena connected with the sea is more interesting, or the effect more enjoyable, than the sea-breeze. Its diurnal, unfailing regularity of recurrence is a wonder and a blessing to mankind. It is felt more or less on the coasts of all maritime countries, many of which deprived of it would be uninhabitable. It commences to blow about 10 A. M., and continues throughout the day to late in the evening. It is caused by the alternate unequal distribution of heat upon the land and sea, or the alternate radiation from those surfaces. It is laden with saline particles, pure, refreshing, and invigorating, toning up the debilitated system, promoting the appetite, and conducing to blissful repose and restorative slumber.

ATLANTIC CITY.

ATLANTIC CITY is called the "City of Homes," having acquired the name by the beauty of the large number of its private cottages. Men of business establish their families here early in the season, and hither return each evening from Philadelphia and other cities, to enjoy the cool repose of their cottage by the sea.

Atlantic City is built on an island ten miles in length, separated from the mainland by a strait called the "Thoroughfare." The hard, smooth strand stretches away in curving lines from Absecom Inlet to Great Egg Harbor Inlet, and at low tide it affords a drive of ten miles along the hard, sandy beach. Twenty-five years ago it was an almost uninhabited island, consisting of a chain of sand hills thrown up by the ceaseless billows. About one-third of the area of the island is now covered with the beautiful city with its broad avenues and streets, which are graded and laid out with good judgment and taste.

Pacific, Atlantic, Arctic, and Baltic Avenues run parallel

with the ocean front: Atlantic being 100 feet wide; Pennsylvania, North Carolina, and Virginia, 80 feet; Pacific, Arctic, and
Baltic, 60 feet; Maine, New Hampshire, Vermont, Rhode Island,
Massachusetts, Connecticut, New Jersey, Delaware, Maryland,
South Carolina, Tennessee, New York, Kentucky, Illinois, In-
diana, Ohio, Michigan, Arkansas, Missouri, Mississippi, Geor-
gia, Florida, and Texas (cross streets), 50 feet in width.

The city is adorned with churches of all denominations,
and contains schools, public and private, and two daily papers.

A city passenger railway traverses the principal avenues,
and several lines of passenger phaetons take passengers to all
parts of the city and island; a number of liveries furnish horses
and carriages for drives at all hours.

THE OCEAN PROMENADE,

or " Board Walk," extends along the entire city front, following
the beach just beyond high-water mark. On a moonlight evening when the beach is crowded with vehicles, and the prome-
nade thronged with pedestrians. Atlantic City then presents a
picture fairer than any vision of a midsummer night's dream.

AMUSEMENTS.

In addition to the customary weekly hops or balls at the
principal hotels, is the Museum, Aquarium, Skating-Rink, etc.
The city is visited during the season by some of the best talent
in music, and concerts and other entertainments are frequently
given. The principal amusements in summer are bathing,
crabbing, and fishing.

SOCIETIES.

Atlantic City has seven societies, viz.: "Trinity Lodge,"
" Pequod Tribe," "American Star Lodge," "Webster Lodge,"
"Seaside Division," "Joe Hooker Post," and " U. S. Fire Com-
pany."

THE THOROUGHFARE.

The thoroughfare is composed of a sheet of water that abounds in the finest fish, oysters, crabs, and clams, and is the rendezvous of the fleet of graceful yachts, in which the visitor can cruise for pleasure or for fishing, either in the smooth water of the inlet or upon the blue briny water of the Atlantic Ocean.

BRIGANTINE BEACH.

A small steamer leaves the Inlet House daily at high tide, the exact time of which is announced in the daily papers and by placards at prominent points for Brigantine Beach. The distance is ten miles through a tide-water course somewhat circuitous. A large hotel is on the beach, facing the ocean, and three hundred yards from the water.

The place has been named North Atlantic City, and in course of time, as its improvements progress, it is proposed to build a railroad to connect Brigantine Beach with Atlantic City, crossing the Inlet by a drawbridge.

Another noted place for visitors is the Absecom Light-house. It is situated on a point of land directly at the mouth of Absecom Bay, where it empties into the ocean. Visitors are admitted only between the hours of nine and twelve o'clock, and without charge. The extreme height of the tower, from base to pinnacle, is 167 feet; to outside gallery, 150 feet, and to focus of lamp 159 feet. The ascent to the gallery is by 228 steps. The light is Fox's hydraulic float fixed light, of the first order, and from the deck of a vessel at sea it can be seen for 26 miles.

SOUTH ATLANTIC CITY.

This elegant beach is free from undertow, making it safe bathing for ladies and children, and also still-water bathing, excellent drinking water, and strict sanitary regulations, insuring health to this new resort.

Among the improvements at South Atlantic City is what is

known as the "ELEPHANT HOTEL," being in shape and anatomy as that well-known animal, and can be seen for miles at sea and the surrounding towns and villages. It is the only building in existence in this novel form, standing in the act of feeding; 86 feet long, 29 feet wide, and 65 feet high, 10 feet diameter of legs, which enclose the stairway, giving an entrance to the body of the animal, which is to be used as a restaurant. There are four side rooms, 6 feet by 8 feet, which will be handsomely decorated. The Houdah or Observatory on the top of the elephant is approached by concealed stairways. The kitchen will be in the head of the elephant.

The railroad has been completed to South Atlantic City by the way of the Camden and Atlantic Railroad, and the surveys have been run by the West Jersey and Narrow-Guage Railroad, and they expect to complete their roads in the shortest possible time, thus giving South Atlantic City the advantage of three railroads. The Camden and Atlantic Railroad Company will run street cars to South Atlantic City at a low rate of fare.

ATLANTIC CITY.

⋙ GEOLOGY. ⋘

THERE is no department of science more interesting to the savant than the geology or cosmic architecture of continents and islands. The geologist and geographer together glean in this most attractive field of scientific research and are rewarded with some of the richest products and enjoy the rarest pleasure vouchsafed to the enthusiastic searcher in the penetralia of nature.

That the relative positions of land and sea are ever changing every observer will admit. Evidences of such changes have been authenticated for thousands of years past, and mountains temples, and cities that once proudly adorned the continental land and the maritime coasts of countries may now be seen submerged by the influent waters or encroachments of the sea, and through the cooperative subsidence of the land upon which they at one time stood. Along the coast of Yorkshire, England, there are shoals or sand-banks in the sea marked as the sites of the towns and villages of Auburn, Hartburn, and Hyde.

The ancient city of Cromer stands submerged upon the floor of the German Ocean, and not far distant, upon the same coast, beneath the water of the ocean, are the ancient villages of Shipden, Wimpnell, and Eccles. The latter submerged village, as if determined that its ancient existence and locality shall not be forgotten or lost, projects aloft above the watery waste the ruined tower of one of its ancient churches, strange and wierd testimony to time's mutations and the impotency of man when measuring strength with the terrible energy of nature.

The voracity of the sea spared not ancient Dunwich, and laid his sacriligious and iconoclastic hand upon her sacred edifices and invaded the ancient mausolea of her dead. In 1740, by submarine explorations, the tombs in the churchyards of St. Nicholas and St. Francis were opened where their coffins and skeletons were exposed to view, the latter lying upon the sands rocked

"In cradle of the rude, imperious surge."

To come nearer home and to have illustrations of the mutations of time, in respect to the ever-changing relation of land and sea, we will cite one instance among many. At Cape May, on the New Jersey coast, the encroachment of the sea was shown by observations made consecutively for sixteen years— from 1804 to 1820, to average about nine feet a year. At Sullivan's Island at the entrance to Charleston Harbor one-fourth of a mile of land has been submerged in the space of three years.

Thus it is evident, proven by incontrovertible facts that the relation of land and sea is ever changing. That there has been, within the memory of man, retrocessions and encroachments and invasions of the sea, at some localities of the maritime coasts of continents, present living citizens of Cape May, Atlantic City, and elsewhere affirm that the coast of New Jersey has undergone such changes and transpositions.

The State of New Jersey, except its northern portion, is alluvial and argillaceous sandstone, post-tertiary. Geologically it is a longitudinal deposit of arenaceous silt contributed by the Delaware River for thousands of years. The sea but comparatively recently covered the present area of the State and the site of Atlantic City. Evidence of such fact is presented by the broad savannahs or meadows that are interposed between the island upon which Atlantic City is built and the high land upon the west. This area of marsh or meadow now almost dry land, if drained and dyked, could be reclaimed and made a profitable area for agricultural and fructiferous purposes.

The island upon which the city is built is a *sand dune*, formed of dry sand and, being permeable, water sinks rapidly through it, leaving a dry surface almost immediately after rains.

This geological peculiarity is one of the agents that contributes to the remarkable healthfulness of Atlantic City at all seasons of the year. There is no indigenous or spontaneous vegetation upon the island. The only growth to be seen is the arboreal embellishments of the avenues and lawns,— sylvan contributions from the forests of the high land. No stagnant pools or sloughs mar or disfigure the facial lineaments of the island, and there is no malarial or miasmatic emanation or effluvium to offend the senses or to affect the perfect hygiene of the city or island.

The city and island only feel the health-giving saline seabreeze flowing in directly from the broad Atlantic Ocean, whose breakers ever and anon lave the glittering strand and whose anthem incessantly ascends to Him who holds the waters of the ocean in the hollow of His hand.

While there is evidence in many places of interchange or transposition of land and sea along the littoral area of the state of New Jersey, the general geographical and topographical limits and features have been preserved, and the lineaments of the landscape have not undergone material alteration, differing but little from its appearance when it was the habitat of its archæological inhabitants. All over the State are vestiges of Indian occupation, and some portions of it are rich treasuries of Indian handicraft in the way of paleolithic and neolithic specimens of savage taste and ingenuity, implements and pottery.

ATLANTIC CITY.

CLIMATE.

SEA AIR.

"Many factors enter into the benefit or good results derived from a residence at the seashore. The principal ones are: The decidedly modified temperature; the toning effect of sea air upon the nervous system; its soporific effects; the inconceivably beneficial effects of sea-bathing.

The breeze coming from the ocean in Summer has a much lower temperature than the land atmosphere. This sea breeze prevails on a large majority of the days during the hot weather, thus making the average summer temperature much lower at the seashore than further inland. On some days the difference is most marked, and few have failed to experience the relief afforded by the first breath of sea air, after spending a hot day in the city. Even when the days are hot, the nights are generally cool. To the invalid, the relief thus afforded from the depressing influence of excessive heat is marked in all cases, but especially is it so in the Summer complaint of children, in the development of which heat plays so important a part. On the other hand, in Winter the temperature of the sea shore is several degrees higher than that inland, owing to the unequal radiation of heat of land and water.

Several elements combine to produce the tonic effect of the sea air. Among these are the following, viz: First. The presence, as shown by Schonbein, of a large amount of ozone; the stimulating, vitalizing principle of the atmosphere. Second. The atmosphere, being denser at the sea level than at more more elevated points, contains in a given space, a larger amount of oxygen. Third. As a larger portion of the breeze comes from the sea, the air contains but a small amount of the deleterious products of decaying vegetable and animal matter. And Fourth. The saline particles held in suspension in the atmosphere, the "dust of the ocean," enter the system through the lungs, and aid in the tonic effect experienced at the sea shore. But whatever may be the cause, the effect is undoubted. Few who visit the sea shore fail to experience a marked improvement in appetite, while to some there comes an intense craving for food, which it seems impossible to satisfy without indulging to an extent bordering on gluttony.

CLIMATE is in intimate relation with the health, wealth, occupation, and longevity of nations. So important are its effects upon the organism of animals that its contemplation or consideration constitutes one of the most engaging and important themes that the mind is invoked to consider.

Many factors contribute to or exercise an influence in the architecture of climate. Proximity and altitude of the land above the sea, average annual mean temperature, local agencies, isothermal relations of the particular locality, relative areas of land and sea, the depth of the adjacent ocean, the general direction of marine currents and winds, radiation, evaporation, annual rain, hail and snow fall, barometrical and electrical states of the atmosphere, deviation and velocity of winds, height, length, and proximity of mountain ranges, are all factors in the make up of the climate of any particular place.

Thus climate embraces a range of subjects and conditions so multifarious as to comprise almost every branch of natural philosophy. It constitutes the aggregate of all the external physical circumstances appertaining to each special locality. The connection between climate and medical science is of inconceivable importance. Hippocrates, the father of medicine, demonstrated that the phenomena of life are not the result of original organization only, but that the moral, intellectual, and physical capacities of man are subject to the influence of these causes, the aggregate of which constitutes climate.

Such investigations tend to show that between the corporeal attributes and intellectual faculties of man and the cosmic conditions by which he is surrounded there exists a mutual dependence and harmony.

ATLANTIC CITY.

ISOTHERMAL RELATIONS.

It is now well ascertained that zones of equal warmth, both upon the sea and land are neither parallel to the equator nor to each other, and it is well known that the *mean* annual temperature may be the same in two places which enjoy very different climates. The seasons may be nearly uniform or violently contrasted. The lines of equal temperature do not coincide with those of equal annual heat, or are not isothermal lines.

On comparing the two continents, Europe and America, it is found that the mean temperatures differ upon the same line of latitude as much as 17° of Fahrenheit. The temperature of Edinburgh, Scotland, is that of localities 800 miles further South. Upon the line of 30° of latitude the difference in temperature in Europe and America is nearly 5°, and upon the parallel of 40° the difference in the temperature of the two continents is 11°. Upon the parallel of 50° Europe has a temperature of 40°.90 and America 37°.94.

Thus we find at New York the summer of Rome and the winter of Copenhagen; at Quebec the summer of Paris and the winter of Petersburg; at Pekin, China, located upon the same parallel as London, the scorching heat of summer is greater than at Cairo, Egypt, and the winters are as rigorous as those of Norway and Sweden. In Van Diemen's Land, corresponding nearly in latitude to Rome, the winters are milder than at Naples, and the summers not warmer than those of Paris, which is 7° farther north. The mean annual temperature of Iceland, situated almost within the Arctic circle, differs but slightly from that of the Orkney and Shetland Islands and the continental land of Scotland.

These peculiarities of climate upon the same or differing parallels of latitude are produced by the vast bodies of water of the circumfluent seas. The continental coast of North America is influenced also to a wonderful degree by the adjacent trending of that wonderful inter-oceanic river of tepid water, the Gulf Steam. This powerful current has a temperature of 7° above that of the surrounding water of the ocean.

This river of warm water, starting from the Carribean Sea, issues from thence through the Bahama Straits, at a velocity of about four miles an hour. It trends along the coast of the southern portion of the North American continent, affecting the temperature of this climate, where in the latitude of Cape Hatteras it is seventy miles broad, and is diverted in a north-east direction. In the latitude of New Foundland it crosses the North-Atlantic ocean to the west coasts of Europe, and pursues its course as far north as Spitzbergen, traversing in its course

over three thousand miles, and from the propinquity of its flow
to the islands of England, Ireland, and Scotland mollifies the
climate of the European continent and islands, and causes
that continent which would otherwise be uninhabitable and
barren, to be habitable and fructiferous.

It is owing to the proximity of flow of this vast warm current to the coast line of this portion of the State of New Jersey
and the locality of Atlantic City that such benignity of climate
is enjoyed by the latter. It causes thermal vicissitudes to be of
less degree of intensity, and atmospheric changes to be more
gradual, depriving such alterations or changes of temperature of
sudden violence of shock to the inhabitant or invalid.

The sea preserves everywhere a *mean* temperature which
it communicates to the contiguous land, so that it tempers the
climate, mollifying alike the heat or cold littorally, and that
of the adjacent land to some extent interiorly.

In consequence of the more equal temperature of the
waters of the ocean, the climate of islands and continental
coasts differs essentially from that of the interior of continents.
The more maritime climates being characterized by mild winters, and more temperate summers. The sea breeze both
moderates the cold of winter and the heat of summer.

It is on account of the propinquity of this body of warm
water, the configuration of the coast, and the topographical
lineaments of the land, the absence of adjacent mountain
ranges that this portion of the New Jersey Coast upon which
Atlantic City is located is so mild and equable in temperature,
and that causes it isothermally to differ with localities upon
the same parallel of latitude, thereby imparting to it a benignity of climate in widely distant and differing localities. Thus in
winter the temperature of Atlantic City is nearly that of
Charleston, and far more equable, in summer the range of the
thermometer is never as high as at New York or Boston ; it is
these peculiar advantages that cause Atlantic City to be so desirable a residence for the invalid either in winter or summer.

ATLANTIC CITY AS A HEALTH RESORT.

ATLANTIC CITY has already acquired widespread fame as a resort for the sick, in both Summer and Winter. It is specially famous as a Winter Sanitarium The Gulf-Stream seemingly comes with the warm South wind, keeping back the fierce blasts of the West, while the solemn sea is always full of strength and health-giving vigor.

The influence of the Gulf Stream undoubtedly has very much to do with it. The warm Gulf-Stream sweeps inward toward the coast of South Jersey, describing a curve whose convexity is nearest the shore in this vicinity. North of Atlantic City it turns sharply to the eastward leaving Long Branch and New York far from its genial influence.

Whatever the influences are that surrounds it, it has a climate unexcelled by that of any other resort in America, with the possible exception of some in Southern California.

Considering the important qualities of purity, dryness, equableness, and mildness of temperature without enervating warmth. no other place on the Atlantic sea-board, at least, can compare with it. Florida is warmer, but hot climates are not found most beneficial either to exhausted nerve centres or diseased lungs. While in summer, the mercury rarely rises above 80°, in winter it rarely falls much below the freezing point. The means of the maximum temperatures for the months of November, December, January, February, and March, 1879, averaged 46.4. The sandy soil is so porous, that any ordinary rain is immediately absorbed, leaving the ground on the beach and elsewhere, except on the much traveled streets, as dry a few hours afterwards as before. Snow is seldom seen. When snow does fall here, it usually vanishes in a day or two; often in a few hours.

The temperature is sufficiently warm to permit invalids to walk or drive out for some hours every day in the week. A sunny sky, dry soil, and genial sea breezes conspire to tempt even the most confirmed hypochondriac to forsake the debilitating confinement of a close, warmed room, and live more out of doors. This is half the battle in most cases. When this is accomplished, tonics and soporifics may be dispensed with, for appetite and sleep come of themselves. Such a climate is found in its perfection, on the Riviera, along the northern shore of the Mediterranean, whither consumptives are sent from all over Europe and America.

ATLANTIC CITY AS A WINTER SANITARIUM.

The reputation of Atlantic City as a winter sanitarium is increasing with remarkable rapidity, as is practically shown by the presence here during the winter season of hundreds of visitors or permanent guests at the hotels and cottages that remain open. Invalids and convalescents suffering from diseases from which it is most difficult to obtain relief, come here in midter and undergo a recuperation that is wonderful. The quickest and most direct cures appear to be effected in complaints springing from nervous exhaustion, though the improvement of those suffering from throat and lung troubles is also remarkable. There seems to be in the very atmosphere something that is hostile to physical debility, and a knowledge of the fact is rapidly becoming widespread through the multiplicity of proofs that are continually being given.

Eminent physicians in New York, Philadelphia, and other cities are constantly sending patients here and seeing them restored to health or greatly improved, after medicines had ceased to benefit them at home. Hundreds of such physicians have both spoken and written in the most flattering terms of Atlantic City air. A striking evidence of its curative power is seen in the wonderful development of business at the hotels during the winter and spring months in the last three years. Previous to 1877 very few strangers were seen in the town before April, and not a great many then. Last year the principal winter houses were crowded before the end of February, and remained so during the entire spring. Most of the guests were invalids or convalescents coming from the wealthier classes in New York, Philadelphia, Baltimore, Washington, Pittsburgh, and Chicago, and were ordered here by their physicians expressly to obtain the benefits of the air.

ATLANTIC CITY.

SPECIAL THERAPEUTIC FEATURES.

WHAT DISEASES ARE BENEFITED.

Of Interest to Invalids and Physicians.

CHANGE of air is a very important medicinal agent. and combined with the other means employed, often enables the physician to effect a speedy cure of cases that would otherwise be of tedious recovery, or it may be, go on to a fatal termination. A change to the more equable temperature, and pure air of the sea-shore exerts at times a truly magical influence upon invalids. The air in passing over the surface of the ocean comes to the shore washed of its impurities and laden with ozone. Sea air strengthens the vital process and stimulates the nervous system, and from the more rapid oxidation of tissue the appetite is improved, and the energy of the muscles revived. Patients who could scarcely walk at home, after coming to the sea-shore, stroll long distances on the strand with only a cheerful sense of weariness that soon passes away, and is succeeded by a sharpened appetite, the reward of agreeable exercise. An abundant supply of nerve food, so essential in the conservation

of force is thus acquired without the whip and spur of tonic bit-
ters, and stimulating stomachics. Physicians are aware that
while the sea-air is not a panacea, it is frequently the "one
thing needful," and especially for "chronic laryngeal and bronchial affections; asthma; disorders of the digestive organs,
with the various forms of dyspepsia ; chronic gout and rheuma-
tism; functional derangements of the generative organs; affections of the kidneys; is beneficial to strumous delicate children;
is invaluable as a restorative during convalesence from acute or
prolonged disease : and especially is it one of the chief resour-
ces of preventive medicine.

DISEASES MOST BENEFITED BY THE AIR OF ATLANTIC CITY.

"Nervous affections decidedly predominate. Every phase of
neurosthenia or nervous exhaustion is represented, from the
comparatively slight indisposition of the society people, worn
out with the season's round of parties and receptions, and the
more threatening depression of vital force often affecting over-
taxed brain-workers, to brain-softening and the worst forms of
paralysis. Dr. S. Weir Mitchell, the eminent neurologist, sends
a large number of his patients here. Besides the nervous diseases proper there is represented the long list of chronic affections, which result secondarily from nervous exhanstion. Next
in order comes the patient suffering from pulmonary, bronchial,
and laryngeal complaints, most of whom are benefited. Many
of these spend the whole winter here, with unequivocal benefit
from an occasional sojourn of a month or six weeks as a change
from the mountains or inland resorts.

"To another class of cases, Atlantic City offers relief, if
not positive cure, which cannot be obtained in any portion of
our sea-coast.

"They are those trying and refractory cases of chronic

bronchitis, laryngitis, incipient tuberculosis, and also scrofula.

" In this respect Atlantic City offers a striking analogy with Nice, where it is well known, all the invalids of Europe (affected with chest-diseases) flock for a winter's sojourn."

WHAT THE CLIMATE OF ATLANTIC CITY DOES FOR SICK CHILDREN.

The " Children's Seashore House " is a handsome cottage erected some years ago on the beach. The object of this institution is to give the benefits of sea-air and sea-bathing to invalid children of Philadelphia and its vicinity as may need them, but whose parents cannot meet the expenses at a boarding house, and often necessary medical advice. They are here under the care of a resident physician, a corps of nurses, and a matron. The total charge, including board, washing. medical attendance, bathing, etc., is not over two dollars per week. This institution has cared for over 2000 patients. In addition to the main building sixteen small cottages have been built in the front, accommodating in all about ninety children with their attendants. An institution for invalid women under much the same management has been built.

" Few of the children who have been admitted to the institution have failed to show, almost immediately, this increase of appetite, and it is, indeed, no exaggeration to say that the effect of the sea-air, in this respect, has been more uniform, and more powerful, than that of any therapeutic agent.

"A very grateful effect of the sea-air upon the invalid is the influence which it frequently has in inducing sleep. Many sick children brought to the institution have slept the first night better than for many nights before. The weariness from the journey has doubtless had some little influence in these cases. but the effect continued. Many, even of those who are not invalids, feel, after a few day's stay at the seashore. unusual drowsiness in the daytime, and the afternoon nap becomes an almost irresistible luxury."

Extracts from the Medical Journals.

The following extracts from articles contributed by physicians to prominent medical journals concerning the effect of sea-air, especially that of Atlantic City, on certain classes of diseases, are particularly noteworthy, being voluntary testimony based upon their personal experience, and written for the exclusive information of their professional brethren.

ATLANTIC CITY.

Dr. J. Walker, of New York City, read before the Medical Society of King's County, N. Y., an elaborate paper on "The Therapeutical Value of Sea-Air in the Diseases of Children," a summary of which has appeared in the *Half-Yearly Compendium of Medical Science.* This paper contained the following, which includes a significant comparison between the advantages of Atlantic City and other seaside resorts :

"The tonic properties of sea-air are due, 1st. To the saline particles found in the spray or ' dust of the sea,' and which are carried hither and thither by the winds and waves ; and 2d. To the freshness of the sea-breeze, which is at its best, when blowing from a good point over a large extent of open sea when it has not been confined by any obstacle or has not been mixed in its passage with any deleterious exhalations," or is not much dampened by rain-fall. These are advantages special to Atlantic City, and cannot be found at any other seaside locality.

Dr. Boardman Reed, of Atlantic City, contributed to the *Medical and Surgical Reporter*, of January 10, 1880, a communication on "Sea-Air for Malaria," from which we extract as follows:

"It may seem like presumption in one practicing in a non-malarial district—at a health-resort, where intermittents do not originate, and can only be studied, as a rule, in the persons of visitors and returning sailors—to express an opinion upon the treatment of this class of affections; yet I venture to make the assertion that even the least efficient of the alkaloids of Peruvian bark will accomplish more, even in moderate doses, when combined with certain other drugs, such as opium, capsicum, leptandrin, gelsemium, etc., than will the sulphate of quinia alone, in the most heroic doses. This statement I have seen verified both in Philadelphia and Atlantic City.

*   *   *   *   *   *   *

Among the invalids sent hither from Philadelphia, New York, and other cities, there are many cases of the malarial cachexia. These often improve amazingly without any medicine, the sea breezes laden with the alterative compounds of chlorine, bromine, and iodine (iodine, by the way, I have found to possess real power over intermittents), proving sufficiently curative.

The liver is the organ chiefly at fault usually, in such cases, and mild remedies which stimulate it gently, at the same time that they promote appetite and digestion, frequently accomplish more than quinine, or even than a too protracted administration of arsenic at least, under the favorable influences here existing. Cases of malarial cachexia which resist all sorts of treatment in the cities, may get well with very little medicine if sent to some non-malarial locality upon the sea-shore."

Eminent Medical Testimonials.

Among the eminent Philadelphia physicians who bear testimony to Atlentic City's value as a winter sanitarium are

JOSEPH LEIDY, M. D.,

Professor of Anatomy, University of Pennsylvania,
1302 Filbert Street.

He says:—" I am pleased to give my testimony as to the healthness of Atlantic City as a place of resort. I know of no place better adapted to invalids in general."

JOSEPH PANCOAST, M. D.,

Emeritus Professor of Anatomy, Jefferson Medical College,
Also says:—" If we had not Atlantic City to go to, we should be at a loss to know what to do with some of our pulmonary and infantile patients."

J. L. LUDLOW, M. D.,

1901 Chesnut Street.

" My opinion of it as a seaside resort, both for pleasure and health, is very high. The air is at all times bracing, and during the winter and fall seasons the effect of the *air alone*, on weak and nervous people is wonderful. I have recommended it and am doing so constantly to our brain-wearied men, and nervous, delicate females, who cannot sleep and have lost their appetites."

WILLIAM DARRACH, M. D.,

Germantown, Philadelphia.

" For the last sixteen years I have been advising patients to go to Atlantic City. I cannot recall a case that has not received benefit from a sojourn there.

It was of great service in restoring tone to the digestive organs of a case of phthisis during the months of January and February. In cases of summer complaints in young children marked beneficial results have followed. Convalescents from typhiod fever and bronchial troubles, especially during the spring months, have been completely restored to health there."

BALTIMORE, October 24, 1881.

I have been an annual visitor to Atlantic City for fifteen years, and have never failed in being benefited, and entirely relieved of dyspepsia, and a troublesome bronchial affection. The air is pure, dry, saline, and genial, soothing to the lungs and tonic to the system. As a winter residence it has no superior.

EPHRAIM LARRABEE.

BALTIMORE, October 10, 1881.

A sojourn at Atlantic City a portion of two seasons has convinced me of the extraordinary hygienic benefits to be derived, in bronchial and pulmonary irritation and morbid sensibility to atmospheric changes. Its equable climate and genial atmosphere affords instantaneous relief.

JOHN T. KING, M. D.

We append also the following list of physicians, including the names of many of the most eminent in Philadelphia, who have endorsed the merits of Atlantic City as a health resort :

Horatio C. Wood, M. D., Professor of Materia Medica, University of Pennsylvania.

D. Hayes Agnew, M. D., Professor of Surgery, University of Pennsylvania.

Walter F. Atlee, M. D.

Frank Woodbury, M. D., Physician to German Hospital, Philadelphia.

Joseph Leidy, M. D., 1302 Filbert Street.

J. C. Guernsey, M. D., Corresponding Secretary Homœopathic Medical Society of Pennsylvania.

John V. Shoemaker, M. D., 1031 Walnut Street, Physician in charge of the Pennsylvania Free Dispensary.

Joseph Pancoast, Emeritus Professor of Anatomy, Jefferson Medical College.

www.ingramcontent.com/pod-product-compliance
Lightning Source LLC
Chambersburg PA
CBHW021458090426
42739CB00009B/1777